Brent Heighton *Artist*

TERRA BELLA PUBLISHERS CANADA INC.

Brent Heighton

Brent Heighton *Artist*

Written by Brent Heighton
& Ken Budd

Cover painting: Powder White

Brent Heighton - *Artist*

published by Terra Bella Publishers
Canada Inc.
604-926-2237
e-mail info@terrabellapublishers.com
www.terrabellapublishers.com
All rights reserved.
Copyright Terra Bella Publishers 1997
Printed in Canada

Canadian Cataloguing in Publication Data:
Heighton, Brent, 1954 -
Brent Heighton

ISBN 1-896171-17-6

1. Heighton, Brent 1954 I. Budd, Ken,
1942 2 Title.
ND 1843.H44A35 1997 759.11 C97-910501-3

Brent Heighton wishes to thank
everyone who has supported his career
through the years. He dedicates this book
with extra special appreciation to
his wife Betty.

Brent Heighton *Artist*

Contents

Brent Heighton

Biographical Background

I was born in Vancouver in 1954. My sister, Roberta, preceded me by twelve years and my brother, Jim, by a decade. At five, my family relocated to Pitt Meadows, then a rural community in the Fraser Valley of British Columbia. My father was a long-time employee for BC Hydro, while my mother dedicated herself to her family.

Our new home was a hobby farm, and we truly enjoyed the country life. There was an orchard of apple, pear and cherry trees, hazelnut trees and blueberry, strawberry and raspberry patches. We got gallons of fresh milk and cream from our very productive cow, and there were lots of geese and chickens roaming the yard. I was often sent to our sizeable garden to retrieve fresh vegetables to feed the dozens of extended family members and other friends who would drop in on sunny summer days and stay for dinner.

Brent Heighton

The Farm

The small farm was surrounded by property that had been logged years before, leaving log bridges over creeks and log roads through marshy areas that, as a young explorer, were great paths to adventure. Our own place had stands of big evergreens.

The farm also had its own swimming hole, a spring-fed pond that my grandfather transformed into a pool by hauling in huge rocks and cementing them together, and then laying in a bottom of sand. The spring kept it fresh, but occasionally, we would drain it and dig out all the dead leaves. Even before we were out of school for summer holidays and right into the next fall's school term, my chums and I would play for hours in the swimming hole.

I had to walk a mile down a country road each day to go to school. As with everything when you're younger, the distance seemed farther, just as the house and the farm seemed bigger.

The only wild creature I tamed, besides a rangy billy goat from down the road, was a raccoon. He was a great magnet for attracting girls. Anytime I went to the park with 'Bandit', the girls would immediately invite me over.

For a brief time, I had a horse called 'Mouse'. She was dapple grey and part-Arab, part-Welsh pony. Our initial meeting was a memorable one. I had been bugging my parents for a long time about wanting a horse, and when they finally gave in and brought 'Mouse' home, she bucked me off the first time I got on her. I wasn't so sure I wanted a horse after that. In fact, I wouldn't go near her for awhile. Then I got tired of everyone telling me I was a chicken, so I met the challenge head on.

My dad would saddle her daily just in case I was ready to try riding again. I had heard that if a horse could put its head down, it could buck, so to keep her head up – I tied a short rope from her bridle to the saddle horn. I also tied another short rope from a front leg to a back leg to keep her from running. I got on and let her limp her way out to a field. If she'd have chosen to go

Bandit

ballistic, I'm sure she would have rolled over on me, but within minutes, I was hollering for my mother to come and see how good I was riding. Mom, the ever-enthusiastic encourager, ignored the ridiculous way I had hobbled the poor horse and complimented me on how good I was doing. After that, 'Mouse' and I were inseparable, galloping for hours around the cow pasture.

My mother constantly encouraged me in most everything I did, especially when I drew. She appreciated the humor in my drawings. My father's reaction to my creations was more along the lines, "You can't make a living drawing cartoons."

My siblings had grown up and left home so my father decided to take a leave of absence from his work. He sold the farm and moved us to southern Ontario to be near my sister who had relocated and started her own family.

As we drove past Kenora and Thunder Bay over the Canadian Shield, I felt relieved that I could call this beautiful new land my home. But then we came to the industrialized cities in the south of the province, and my heart sank. Gone were the wild woods and semi-wilderness of my youth.

We settled in Dresden, Ontario, and I entered high school as a stranger to everyone around me. Fortunately, through my doodling, I had developed a knack for doing caricatures. Soon I had kids asking me to do a cartoon of them, or a friend or teacher. It was my ticket to popularity, and the beginning of a positive experience that forced me to rely on my own abilities and deal with the fears connected to this new adventure.

I enrolled in a grade eleven art class taught by Mrs. Suderman. Freda Suderman loved her work, and I guess she considered me a work in progress. She took me under her wing.

I was always eager to get to her class, and was embarrassed – yet secretly proud – when she would pay me additional attention, using my work as an example in front of the class, or encouraging me to draw a specific assignment yet again, from another angle or perspective. She showed concern. She made me work hard. She knew how to inspire me.

We all hopefully have a teacher or two we remember as having had a remarkable influence on our lives, such as Mrs. Suderman had on mine. It was while under her tutelage, that I recognized that painting was to be my great passion. I graduated from high school and floated for awhile. I came back to British Columbia that summer and traveled around, working in construction. When I returned to Ontario, I took a job in Chatham in the suspension division of a factory that made springs for cars and trucks. In the course of my work, I discovered 'paint sticks', a kind of wax-like bar like an oil pastel that was used to number and code pieces that came off the assembly line. When you touched the stick to the side of one of the hot furnaces in the plant, the colour flowed from it as if it was a magic wand. And there were dozens of brilliant colours to choose. With my penchant for doing cartoons and caricatures, my love of humor and my new-found weapons, I waged war on the drab black of the furnaces in the factory. Within weeks, I had the entire place looking like Disneyland had collided with a paint factory!

One day a memo appeared on the bulletin board announcing the visit of a committee of major shareholders. It also pronounced that the factory was going to receive a new paint job. And there was an added paragraph that said, "We appreciate Mr. Heighton's artistic talent, but we feel he should be expressing his ability elsewhere."

While the edict was a warning I could lose my job, it was also public recognition that I should consider a career in the arts. It made me think. I was making good money, but did I really want to work in a factory for the rest of my life?

By the end of that year, I had moved to Ottawa, begun working part-time in the shipping department of a furniture store, and painted landscape and architectural watercolours in my spare time. I was enrolled in arts courses at Algonquin College. My original plan was to sign up for the commercial art program, because I believed I would find it easier to make a living at commercial art, but when I showed the department head examples of my work, he steered me directly into the fine arts program.

As a way of making some additional money, I went to a craft fair at Carleton University and assembled my easel to sketch caricatures of people on the spot. A man sat down in the chair opposite me, and while I was determining the best way to represent him, a crowd gathered around. Absolute panic set in.

Fortunately, my subject had a huge nose, was fully bearded and had bizarre hair, so he was easy to 'do'. Once I got started on the task, all peripheral distractions disappeared, and I went to work. In minutes, I was finished and had three dollars in my hand. By the end of the day, my revenue had risen to over fifty.

That got me started. I was earning enough creating caricatures to pay my tuition and buy art supplies. I stayed in the fine arts program on a part-time basis for a couple of years, continuing to do caricatures on the side, all the while developing a pretty good hand and establishing my ability with the brush. I had evolved from initially doing cartoons with pencil, to using felt pens, and ultimately brushes.

Of equal importance in many ways was the realization I could make money in the art business. A constant yearning I had for the west coast finally won out, and in 1976, I moved back to Vancouver. Selling men's wear brought in some money, but to top up my financial reserves, I fell back on my skill of creating caricatures and set up shop in Stanley Park along with other artists at the entrance to the zoo. I added a twist to my new circumstance by also selling my paintings – some oils, mostly watercolours.

The more I painted, the more I wanted to learn about painting. I visited Douglas College, where I stirred up a bit of a commotion with the bureaucrats in admissions. I was again interested in graphic arts, because I believed it would help me to develop my technical abilities, but I also wanted to study more life drawing, which was offered by the fine arts department. The advisor was set on having me understand that I couldn't be in both programs at the same time. The more she persisted, the more I kept requesting even more courses that crossed departmental boundaries. Completely exasperated, she finally told me that I could not expect to get credit for any courses if I chose to hopscotch between the two programs. A deal was immediately struck.

For the next two years, I audited courses at all levels of both programs part-time, while drawing and painting, often in Stanley Park, for several hours a day – practicing, practicing, practicing. I also used the knowledge gained in some of my commercial art courses to make additional money doing animation projects and illustrations. I had succeeded in designing an educational experience to meet my own needs, sacrificing the piece of paper that would say I was a graduate.

When I was twenty-four, I met the love of my life, my wife, Betty. The commitment resulted in an instant family in that I acquired a wonderful six-year old daughter. Terri is Betty's child from a previous marriage, and I luckily gained the love of two exceptional females at the same time. In another nine years, our family would grow by one more when Julie, our second beautiful daughter, would be born. Betty worked part-time for the first few years of our marriage, and by combining our incomes, we happily survived. Betty's support has always been there. I had taken everything I

*Brent, Betty and the girls
on holiday in Rome*

*Brent at a
workshop*

could at Douglas College, so I began to explore art workshops. The first was with Rex Brandt of the National Academy of American Watercolourists Society, whose work I had seen and admired in numerous art magazines. His wife, Joan Irving, was also a celebrated artist, and together they came to Vancouver to give a workshop.

A significant insight I gained from interacting with many older artists and instructors at workshops was that they all wished they would have committed to the goal of art when they were much younger. They felt they had wasted too much time traveling other paths. Their honesty made me determined not to make the same mistake.

Under the umbrella of the Federation of Canadian Artists, and the co-sponsorship of the Federation Gallery in Gastown, Allen Edwards, a Vancouver artist, encouraged a number of younger painters to plan and participate in *The Saltspring Seminar*. The camaraderie of sharing several days under the tutelage of established artists, such as Edwards, Harry Heine and Bill Reese from the States, was a hallmark experience. We enjoyed an inspirational day with each artist/instructor, always at a different location, and then would continue in the evening, staying up until all hours to discuss the art. The Federation flourished, offering an ongoing network for artists to gather and share, and staging art exhibitions, such as the Under 30 show where I would display my work. It was an exciting and stimulating environment, with sincere involvement and fantastic optimism.

Workshops have been a way for me to rejuvenate, to explore new options, and to learn. The positive sum of all of those experiences is the reason that I have been offering workshops for over a

Brent with a student

decade where I am committed to helping people develop their creativity – especially through practice, practice, practice. Initially, I was not happy with my art unless I could differentiate between each blade of grass in a field I had painted. Realism was my touchstone. It seemed that as I became competent with a specific technique, I became tired of it. I took risks to attempt different kinds of artistic styles. I found I liked to work in abstract.

It has been a bumpy ride over a long period of time to arrive at this point. I liken it to the uncertainty of Charles Lindberg's quest to be the first flyer to wing his way across the Atlantic. You get the plane off the ground – somewhat of an accomplishment in itself – and reach an altitude where you feel everything's under control. But then there are a series of mechanical concerns or foul weather systems that constantly test your mettle and cause you to question the wisdom of your choice to set such a lofty goal. And wherein I haven't landed my plane successfully yet, at least I'm still aloft, and the propeller keeps on churning! While there has been – and I suspect will continue to be – constant hurdles to overcome, I have been extremely fortunate. It has not been all that difficult to keep a positive outlook towards my work. When a new blanket of snow smothers the countryside, I am inspired. When the azaleas and rhododendrons burst into bloom in my garden and my Koi fish reappear, I'm keen to paint. The angles of branches in a forest or the way the light streams through them can cause me to rush to my studio. A weathered fence, a golf green, fishboats in a harbour, intriguing architecture, waterfowl on a pond: all or any can move me to paint. And when I am painting, I am happiest.

- Brent Heighton
(with Ken Budd)

The Art of

Brent Heighton

Floral Paintings

I get a significant amount of pleasure from my Koi pond. So much so, that it has served as both inspiration and subject for many paintings. I love the solitude it presents. It is an amazingly peaceful place to gather my thoughts.

I love its uniqueness. The shapes of the fish under the water and the surrounding water plants lend wonderful forms that give balance to my paintings. And then there are the extraordinary colours, not only within the distinctive patterns on the fish, but the astounding pinks and mauves of the azaleas and rhododendrons that border the pond and Japanese garden.

I would hope everyone could have a quiet place, be it a pond or a glade in a forest, where they can find solace and beauty.

For me, painting an orchid is about two things: the patience required to observe and nurture its growth, and the tactile sense awakened by this beautiful flower. As you watch the bud swell, you become entranced with its development. It becomes a part of your world and you invest time in it. You must have patience, but through the process, you seem to gain a form of power.

Then it reaches full bloom, and the magnificent blossom of the orchid has reached its full potential. Its beauty is radiant, its elegance reminding me somehow of a Spanish dancer swirling and twirling in a gorgeous gown of white, with just a hint of golden colour in its centre. Touching that satin shape is delightfully sensuous.

Powder White

Koi Pond

There are a number of positive aspects to painting still life. It allows the artist to combine colours and shapes that might not otherwise exist in real life. This makes it a great way to train the artist to explore subjects – even in nature – and perhaps even manipulate the subject, to arrive at the desired composition.

Ambrosia has a feeling, a certain air of classical imagery to it. The dictionary definition of ambrosia is "food of the gods", but in this instance, I've taken license with the definition to mean "to be pleasured by the opulence of colour and its use". Still life studies can give you that.

Tea Pot & Flowers as part of our lifestyle is a pretty typical thing. We enjoy a daily pot of tea (and now they've proven it's good for us). We often adorn our homes with flowers – daisies, lilies, irises and the like. Neither act seems terribly special. But, if we give it some thought, I suspect we would more greatly appreciate these little things in life.

Technically, I placed the daisies directly in the centre of the painting, which is contrary to the recommended norm, and used the spiky portions of the foliage – the leaves and the twigs – to surround the daisies, as if to suspend them in space. The colours of the other floral arrangement in the upper corner eventually pull the viewer's eye away from this "dead centre" focus.

From an artist's perspective, these still lifes allow us to be challenged and to manage the subject we choose to paint. We can even leave the painting arena for a time and come back to revisit the project later.

Ambrosia

Teapot & Flowers

Fishing Paintings

Tranquil Cove

As an artist, I am aware that observation — true *seeing* — can happen anywhere, any time. It never shuts off, but I have to be cognizant of its availability, of its opportunity, and, perhaps most importantly, of its power.

I painted the fly fisherman series vertically because it emulates the shape seen in oriental paintings, a shape that is ethereal and spiritual. Back lighting accentuates this. I was also trying to emphasize the use of the shape, the feeling of awe that height and space gives. The trees on the edges of the streams and the mountains in the background adds to the feeling of power and quiet strength. In *Cold Stream*, however, I attempted to capture the breadth a horizontal image can offer and the extreme distances to which the fisherman's delicate line can reach.

Whenever I take a moment for introspection and allow myself to absorb the elixir offered by the natural world, I am constantly amazed at how insignificant man is in the total scheme of things. I can't sit by a lake or a stream in the folds of a mountain without feeling we are but a single cog in a very large wheel. Nature is powerfully inspirational to me.

So, too, are the arts – painting, sculpting, music and dance.

The first time I saw a fly fisherman plying the eddies of a quiet river for his elusive, finned prey, I recognized a marriage between art and nature. I see the action of the fly fisherman's line, as it floats on gentle breezes, as a soothing, rhythmic ballet. It is an entwining of man with nature that is completely harmonious, the swaying of the line perhaps even a metaphor for a soft wind.

Cold Stream

Trout Haven

As with mountainscapes – and probably with every painting I do – the shapes within the image can be directly responsible for a successful outcome. Often, as in the case of *Morning Fog*, the shapes I incorporated came not only from objects or subjects within the painting, but were achieved through the use of light forms. In this particular case, I used a lot of back lighting, attempting to create the impression that the boats sitting in the harbour were nestled on silver paper.

I wanted to exhibit fluid movement in the water, yet to have a quiet calm dominate the scene. Stylistically, I have focused on the use of abstract mostly. The water, the mist and the clouds, even the foliage on the shoreline, contribute to the work's abstract nature. The boats, as well, have a certain amount of abstractness to them. It's within the details on the boats, the beams and the trim, that I utilize realism. The finished result, ultimately, is a representational painting.

Morning Fog

Crossing Over

Crystal Pool

Breaking Off

Takin' the Fly

Seascapes

The Oregon Coast is an amazing place. One day it can be gentle with placid waters and sun-strewn beaches, and the next it can be a boiling rage with rain that comes at you horizontally.

When it's in a passive mode, there's an incredible beauty to it. There's colour in the sky, but often a mist seeps in that permeates everything. The bold strength of the rocks along the shoreline is softened by this wrap of gauze, creating a dichotomy of hard and soft, strong and gentle. You can sometimes see the fog coming – a wall of white rolling towards the shore. Inevitably, winds wipe the beach clean, and then there can be an incredible display of riotous colour or subtle, pastel washes, as sunset descends.

I sometimes sense a fear within me when I decide to attempt a painting of such a dynamic place. Fortunately, that tentativeness is tempered by the excitement of the challenge. In each situation, I try to let the feelings I am given by the environment prevail. It's the feelings that dictate my direction and my intensity.

Regatta began as an abstract painting with no preconceived idea as to what the subject might become. Indeed, it might well have ended there, as a study and statement of form and colour, except during the process of creating movement through shapes and colour, the angularity and interaction of the shapes on the canvas took on a sailing theme. In the end, it turned out to be a representational painting. The success of the painting, for me, is realizing that the excitement was there before the subject matter was revealed.

Like flying an airplane in a cloudbank and not knowing which way is up or down, painting can be extremely chaotic at times. It's wonderful to feel there is possibility amidst that chaos, and to truly enjoy that process. Abstract painting is the simplifying of forms, and it is an excellent exercise for developing your creativity and powers of observation. Instead of seeing things, you are creating relationships of shapes and colours and movements. I suspect I will spend the rest of my life trying to learn the reality of that concept.

Regatta

Tide Pools

Landscapes

Many of my mountainscapes focus mostly on creating a variety of shapes within the painting. When I think of mountains, I think in terms of diagonal lines, and in *Tamarack*, I feel I achieved using diagonal lines effectively to represent the mountains in the image. As well, I incorporated vertical height through the inclusion of evergreens, and thirdly, there are the blocks and round shapes of rocks. The ultimate challenge is to take those shapes and lines and blend them harmoniously – often by simplifying them – to arrive at the intended outcome.

In addition to the attention that needs to be paid to the geometrics of a painting, there is the on-going concern for the correct balance of colour, the blending of subtle colours with more powerful ones.

Perhaps the most urgent aspect to the creation is to bring a sense of immediacy, a feeling of freshness, to the painting. I believe that's why I'm such a believer in watercolours, because there is always that urgency and freshness when you are painting in that medium.

I like snow as a subject for my art. It gives me the opportunity to work with amorphous shapes, shapes that appear almost plastic. I can work more in the abstract with these shapes, because they are very light and create intriguing patterns. Snow permits me to push the limits of abstraction and still have the outcome considered representational.

Another wonderful aspect of snow is that when light hits it in certain ways, it splinters into beautiful colours. I look for that kind of stimuli, where I'm given the opportunity to take what's there and expand upon it, or play it down if necessary. But first of all, I feel fortunate to have a chance to see it. Many people think of snow as being blue and white, but within *Frequent Visitor*, I saw the snow as being warm in some areas, cool in others.

Add the factors of shade and shadows with this range of colours and distinct moods are created. When you see light passing through the forest, you discover the underlying structure that helps develop the skeleton that locks everything together.

Loons in the Mist

Tamarack

The dark absorbs, and you get a lot of reflective light and exciting shapes.

As a balance, or perhaps even an antagonist to the character created by the soft, rounded shapes of the snow, I integrate vegetation into the scene. Unlike the reality of a photograph, a painting can have form, shape, texture and a myriad of other things wherever the artist wants it. I chose to make some of the plants lacy, with lots of texture. Others are strong and dominant. Both give a greater essence to the snow, adding interesting shapes and providing more excuses to infuse even more colour into the main subject.

I don't paint wildlife for the sake of painting wildlife. There are many others very capable of doing that, and I have utmost respect for those artists. I attempted to represent the animal as part of nature – within nature. The kingfisher in *Frequent Visitor* and goose in *The Retreat* are there, but not there. They are part of the whole thing, giving scale to the paintings and offering subtle focal points.

The Retreat

In *Sanctuary*, I attempted to convey the emotion we all feel during that special time in. The palette at that time can be extremely strong when the garishness of changing leaves bounces off blue sky, but there is also a more subtle, softer time when a patina of gold, almost an aura, washes over everything like a fine mist. Warmth melds into a golden hue. It is the serenity available in this portion of the palette that I wanted to emulate. I still painted my blues, golds and other colours, but worked at not overstating them.

I am not a hunter, but in the same way I can enjoy the bliss of listening to loons on a lake during the quiet of early evening, I can relate to a hunter hunkered down in cattails and thrilling to the sight of geese coming into the decoys. Like a squadron of aircraft coming in for a landing, the flock of geese spills from the sky, twisting and weaving their way to a slippery landing.

Frequent Visitor

Sanctuary

Driftwood

Serene Morning

Green In Two

Travels

Scenes like *Flower Market* are fun to paint. They offer a juxtaposition of soft, round shapes and vibrant colours with stronger, more powerful, angular aspects of the scene, along with muted, softer colours.

When I think of my visits to the south of France and specifically, the markets of the area, the word *fresh,* seems to embody my thoughts and feelings. Everything is fresh: the freshly-hosed marketplace, the fresh smells of earthy vegetables, the aroma of freshly-made coffee and baguettes, and the almost throbbing, electric colours of freshly-cut flowers. These colours allow the artist to play with the painting, to create a palette with such a dazzling array that in real life you would find such combinations discordant.

In contrast to the soft fluffiness and energetic colours of the flower stands are the stiff, sober shapes and sombre tones of the buildings around the marketplace. The vertical sternness of creamy sandstone buildings streaked by the stains of time give way to the curved, yet sharp angles of awnings that cling to the buildings. It's the intertwining of these elements that brings great joy to the work of interpreting this experience.

Sometimes a mix of things collide to create the opportunity to see a painting that you just have to paint. I suspect this happens more often than I realize. Such was the case when I discovered the subject for *Feeding Time*.

My family and I were visiting at a friend's place in upstate New York. It was a farming area, and having been brought up on a farm, I was already in a mind-set of heightened awareness. To add to that, I had become enthralled with the barns and scenes of country roads in that part of the country.

I was throwing a 'long bomb' during a game of catch on the front lawn with a young lad from the family we were visiting, when, serendipitously, I looked beyond him to notice the wonderful sight I eventually encapsulated in the painting. I had looked at that scene several times while we were playing, but it wasn't until that moment that I *saw* the painting.

Flower Market

Feeding Time

New York, on the other hand, also has a European flavour, but being an American city, it has less history to draw on. It definitely feels different with its own style – Broadway plays, yellow taxis, Jewish delicatessens serving great corned-beef sandwiches. It's very eclectic with distinctive neighbourhoods like Brooklyn and Harlem. It's not the cleanest city I've visited and can be very cluttered, but it's wonderfully resilient.

Travelling is one of my life's great joys. As an artist, it is divinely inspirational. As a person, it's tremendously educational.

After The Rain

Broadway

Come On In

When travelling through Europe, you become aware of the importance given to entrances. Almost every entrance, in even the smallest houses, has an interestingly-shaped door, many with windows in them, and many with beautiful porches over them. Typically, there is a window beside each door with curtains showing behind it. The entrance is then finished with wonderfully textured walls, perhaps a wreath of flowers on the door, and a sitting area near the entrance with the obligatory small table adorned with a vase of flowers. The scene is a painter's dream.

But beyond the magnetic draw of this pleasant scene with its exciting presentation of colour, I see incredible geometric shapes. There are squares that create all sorts of different feelings of movement, and there are rectangles that play off against the curves and circles of the softer, floral images. The tangible objects in the scene are enough to draw a painter to want to capture it, but for me, I'm attracted to the mood created by the relationship and the movement between the shapes.

Brent Heighton

Brent Heighton paints out of his studio in Surrey, British Columbia, Canada, but he travels regularly to find new inspirations and subjects for his paintings as well as to further expand the international interest in his work. In Canada he shows with many galleries and also with the Western Artist's Group which puts on public exhibitions and offers teaching workshops. Brent Heighton's work has been available in limited editions, posters and cards through the Canadian art publisher, Canadian Art Prints for 15 years. The extensive distribution of his images has contributed to making Heighton a highly recognizable and popular artist in Canada and the United States.

Ken Budd

Ken Budd's writing credits include Touch the Magic, Cowboys and Kananaskis Country, Releasing the Light, The Art of Carol Evans. Ken lives on the Sunshine Coast of British Columbia where he continues to pursue writing, publishing and production activities through his company SummerWild Productions.